Angels & Beasts

ISBN 978-1-927496-00-8

Edited and designed by Elizabeth Adams
Cover illustration: detail from "The Last Judgement," a fresco on the exterior
of the Church of St. George, Voroneţ Monastery, Romania, c. 1540.

First Edition

Published by Phoenicia Publishing, Montreal
www.phoeniciapublishing.com

Printed in the United States

Angels&Beasts

Claudia Serea

PHOENICIA PUBLISHING
MONTREAL

Table of Contents

Acknowledgments

Grateful acknowledgment is made to the editors of the following journals, anthologies and presses where some of these poems first appeared, sometimes in earlier versions or under a different title:

The Bicycle Review: *The premonition*
BAP Quarterly: *Myths flying low over the city*
2 Bridges Review: *Longbeak*
Bluestem: *Place your left foot on the folded wings*
Breadcrumb Scabs: *My brother and I emerge victorious, I walked into the woods, The half-man-half-a-limp-rabbit, It's over now, the experiment*
Contrary Magazine: *Bigeye, The snake, The worms*
Flutter: *For a while, an angel lived with me, Some angels walk among us, You turn on the city lights*
Now Culture: *I wake in a clot of darkness, Her back is turned, Always, everything George, I skate on the rim*
Patasola Press: *Dearest little one, A baby goat jumps*
Prick of the Spindle: *She comes in from the rain, Play, play!, The violinist plays, My father reads a burning newspaper, In my grandmother's village*
The Missing Slate: *I rang the doorbell at the top floor apartment*
The prose poem project: *In the deserted delivery room, A man walks, On CNN tonight, Since their white and black feathers look the same at night, Forest, forest, Before she makes pilaf, The red balloon reports the blue one*
RESPIRO: *The neighborhood queen*
Shadowbox: *White as Milk, Gaia, I finally got inside the ear*
Word Riot: *The chicken bones*
wtf pwm 2.3: *The music box, Says the woman, A girl's hand*

The poem *Her back is turned* was nominated for the 2011 Best of the Net and the 2011 Pushcart Prize by *Now Culture*. Many thanks to the editors Don Zirilli and Gene Myers.

12 poems from *The Bank Teller's Name is Jesus* were published as an e-chapbook titled *With the Strike of a Match* (White Knuckles Press, 2011.) Many thanks to the editors Howie Good and Dale Wisely.

The poems from *The Little Book of Answers* were written as responses to Pablo Neruda's *The Book of Questions* and they were first published in *Respuestas—The Neruda Project*. Hats off to the editor of *Respuestas*, Alex Bleeker.

The poem *The neighborhood queen* is forthcoming in the anthology *Gypsies* edited by Mihaela Moscaliuc and Michael Waters.

Many thanks to my teacher Jim Klein. Hats off to Rick Mullin, Jeff McMahon, and Lisa Marie Basile, and to The Red Wheelbarrow Poets for their constant support and friendship. I am fortunate to know you. To Ionut and Dana, va iubesc.

For Dana

There's something I must tell you,
but you don't have to listen.
Of turtle's wings and sticky things
and a tooth of mine that's missing.
Come close so I can whisper
things I don't understand.
And, as I tell my tales
for naughty boys and girls,
please, may I hold your hand?

—Duane Michals,
Upside Down Inside Out and Backwards

I

Angels & Beasts

In the deserted delivery room, the moon came to shine the tools and the steel sink. I was small and quiet as a spoon. *Another girl to bear the world's pain,* my mother said, and the plum tree outside the window dropped a few pink petals.

Bigeye

Bigeye could see the grain of dust in the wind and the flame in coal.
He could see the fish in the sea. He could see the child inside his mother's
womb, the tulip inside the bulb, the sap beneath the bark of trees, the
grubs underground. He could see buried seeds and bones, the grass roots
penetrating the graves.

But people clouded Bigeye's vision. He couldn't see the lies behind
a straight face. Greed was a smudge and love a blur. Bigeye was afraid, so he
went to the doctor and got big eyeglasses. He always wore them. That's how
he spotted the purple spider hanging inside his own left ventricle.

For a while, an angel lived with me in the silence of my room.
He talked to me and covered me with his heavy wings so I could sleep.
We watched the street together, our faces in the window barred by the
shadows of the trees. He wasn't white, but gray, a soft raincloud color.
Love lent him a tint of gray, a taint.

The snake

Unbrother woke up at night and made a clay snake. The snake told him to drown his brother. Brother woke up, caught the snake and threw it in the sky, to wind around the earth nine times and protect it from the flood. You can see it right there: the white snake stretched over the house with all its silver scales.

Yeah, grandma, but what happened to the brothers?
One of them lives in your heart. The other one coils in your belly.

I walked into the woods, and I met Half-man-half-a-limp-rabbit. His paws were dipped in blood. Did he kill someone? Did he testify against his best friend?

Which one is the road home? I asked, but he didn't answer, didn't even look up. I kept walking. Next to me, the Half-man-half-a-limp-rabbit kept limping.

The music box

On the flea market table, there is a snow globe with glittering flakes.
It's a musical box playing a lullaby. The rabbit family gathers inside
around the baby just born. It's my little brother in the crib, with Mommy
and Daddy looking on.

 The snowflakes turn dark as we stare, and soon it snows blood.
Someone shakes the snow globe, and the blizzard of blood covers all of us.

Play, play! the mustached violin teacher yells, banging the bow against the table. The little girl's violin doesn't dare cry. His voice booms in the room as small as a cell: *Faster, goddammit!* The little fingers startle and slip; Kreisler stumbles and falls. The girl's knees shake; her violin plays mosquitoes and bees. *Louder, louder! Play like in hell!*

Outside the barred window, the trees burst into blossom, and thunder rolls into rain.

The chicken bones

Some people could roll over three times and turn into dogs. There were a lot of stray dogs around. They traveled in packs, following us on the sides of the road. Mother always threw them some chicken bones, which bought us just enough time to escape.

There was no escape. Soon, we were the chicken bones that another family on our street threw at the dogs. They, too, were trying to buy time to escape but stumbled, fell, and accidentally rolled over three times, turning into chicken bones that someone else threw at the dogs. That went on for a while, and is still going on today.

Forest, forest, when I think of you,
Forest, forest, I feel young again

My mother irons linens and sings. It's a sad song, for there aren't any forests around. We live across from a cement factory and its mountains of gravel and sand. Mother stacks the ironed tablecloths and bed sheets, all the laundry ironed to a crisp, even the underwear. They line up high cement panels in the gray dusk.

    Forest, forest, she sings, and the dusk grows darker and lasts for almost fifty years.

Some angels walk among us looking just like regular people. Sometimes they even play football, like this guy with a sweaty t-shirt. He takes a long drink of water and looks at me knowingly. When he pulls his shirt overhead, I can see the scars where the wings fasten. I bet he has them neatly folded in the duffle bag he carries after the game.

My father reads a burning newspaper. The letters explode with sounds of shrapnel and dirty his hands. The pages go up in flames. He leaves the paper folded on the table. Black oil drips from the pages and pools on the porch. The cinder, a flock of starlings, flies to the ceiling.

The newspaper is called *The Truth*. It arrives at 6 a.m. in a rusty truck loaded with stacks tied with rope. My father waits in line and pays a few coins to the old lady at the stand. He buys the truth every day and walks back home, carrying it in a plastic bag.

I wake in a clot of darkness. When the third rooster crows,
I hear the werewolf jump over the neighbor's fence. It grunts
and paces outside the door, sniffing out the scent of our dreams.
The werewolf seeps in and eats my father's dreams. But he
can't eat mine. Not while I'm still awake.

In my grandmother's village, there is a deep well. I swear it goes to the center of the earth. I don't bend down to see my reflection, but I speak into it and my voice echoes. The water is salty from underground tears. Sometimes, the moon crawls into the bucket. I throw a coin inside, wishing for something to come true, and the well catches it in its teeth.

Before she makes pilaf, my grandmother sorts the specs of dirt and tiny pebbles out of the rice. She moves her lips as if talking to the grain, or counting it. The rice multiplies and fills the room with white shiny mounds in the moonlight. It will take Grandma a lifetime to sort the dirt out of all this rice, I'm thinking, as I'm looking for my lost baby tooth, the size of a grain.

    Great, now I'll never find it to throw over the house for good luck, I say. Grandma smiles at me, and the rice smiles, too, myriads of baby teeth.

Her back is turned. The head kerchief covers her hair as if she should be ashamed she has any. She keeps stirring the pot on the stove, but I know only chicken feet float in that soup. The dust in the room is a thousand years old and keeps rising to her ankles, to her knees.

The worms

The giant used a huge rake deep across the garden and gathered the worms and grubs in mounds that soon grew into heaps. The giant smashed the worms with his boots.

He drowned some; others he buried in the salt mine. Hundreds of thousands of squirmy worms shoveled, gone. Without them, the land withers and mills into dust, for everyone knows the worms weave the earth and keep it together.

White as milk, the stag carries the souls of dead children.
He drinks the tears from their mothers' eyes and grazes on thin
memory grasses. He stops at the abandoned house to rummage
through the rubble, looking for small clothes. The children's souls
are nestled in silk swings hooked on the stag's antlers. He carries
them gently over treetops and roofs, and into the moon.

Says the woman in the teacher's lounge: *When the great leader died, I cried.*

My father danced, my mother says. I'll never forget it. I was a little girl and watched as he twirled around the yard without a word. He hopped on one foot, then the next, and moved his hands around as if crushing lice with his fingernails.

My brother and I emerged victorious after hours of waiting in line, holding a couple of bags with livid animal feet inside. The chicken feet were called *flatware*, and the pig feet *Adidas sneakers*. Mom will be so proud of us, we thought. On the way home, we counted: four pieces of flatware, two sneakers, enough to eat for a week.

The premonition

I walked into a small, whitewashed room, where the mice had pierced all the walls. I was inside a white piece of cheese with round rat holes everywhere. I'll remember this as long as I live.

I had made *piftie*, garlic meat aspic, and I was carrying it on a white China dish. It quivered and shook with every step I took. I remember saying to myself *I can't leave the platter here—the rats will eat the aspic.* And I turned, and the platter slid right out of my hands. But it didn't break. The meat jelly landed in a trembling mound on the floor; it didn't spatter or spread.

And that's how I knew, Carmen, your pancreas was pierced like a piece of white cheese, but the infection didn't spread in your belly. It gathered in one place, and the doctors scooped it out the way I cleaned the meat jelly from the floor.

The red balloon reports the blue one for its inflated ego. The blue balloon bursts into tears. The yellow one doesn't feel so well, and the white one has a blank stare as my brother ties them all to his backpack.

When the clouds look the other way, the wind steals the balloons and ties them to the tallest tree branch. From there, the balloons can see the sunset and the planes in the sky's belly.

At night, they float with the moon.

The half-man-half-a-limp-rabbit loves me with his half-heart-half-a-rotten-carrot. He speaks in half-truths, goes half the distance, cuts time in half. He likes his coffee with half-and-half and things half-done.

Will I see my husband again? I ask, and his half-mouth laughs.

At the last dinner before the fall, we listen to a radio broadcast telling us everything is under control. Mother sets the table. We sip the soup with bits of bread and talk about school. The stars gather in the sky, holding their wings and tongues, already knowing what we'll find out when the time comes.

It's over now, the experiment that lasted almost 50 years, in which the skin was peeled back and the flesh cleaved to reveal the cobalt spine. This was extracted and replaced with corn mush.

A new experiment started. The lab mice crowd the sterile rooms, pushing to get to the front because they heard the mush is now made of gold. They bribe the cage guards to get to the top of the dissection list. They are willing to trade in other body parts, like their tongue. They wait in line for days before arriving in front of the scientist whose grin looks strangely familiar.

Gaia

Gaia's wings could turn the day into night. Circling the sky,
it followed Grandma everywhere as angels follow people.
When time came, Grandma saw Gaia waiting outside the window.
She tried to warn me, but her voice was garbled. In an instant,
Gaia was inside the room. It swooped down, grabbed Grandma's
breath and flew off, leaving behind a whirlpool of red petals.

II

The Little Book of Answers

Will our life not be a tunnel
between two vague clarities?

Or will it not be a clarity
between two dark triangles?

Or will life not be a fish
prepared to be a bird?

—Pablo Neruda,
The Book of Questions

I send you transparent love letters that barn swallows sow in the sky when I miss you. The swallows are great mail carriers: they fly fast and low, preserving the letters' sentiments. Sometimes their job makes them late for school, and they get punished: they have to sit for hours on a wire and sing in unison.

Death is a flower pressed in a book. Death is the book and its pages, the emperors and presidents. The history professor teaches death every day, so why wouldn't the geography teacher? Death is pressed between canyon bedrocks. The mountains are filled with death, the deserts move sands of death, and the rivers carry death in their bellies. Even the weather is volatile death swirling in the atmosphere. The geography teacher doesn't really have a choice.

Yes, the crickets pierce holes into the night's hat. The wind steals it
and gives it to the trees who wear it until dawn.

Dance now,
says the old ash to the fire.
Soon, you'll die,
and everything you have will be mine.

There is one bee for every child. When I was in first grade, a bee fell from a dogwood tree under my collar. It tickled, so I twitched. The bee dipped its needle into the side of my neck and died. My neck swelled and hurt badly. Ms. Aldea rubbed it with salt and chopped parsley, and assured me the pain will pass by the time I marry.

I guard under my shell a pair of wings, says the turtle,
for I work as an angel on weekends.

The oranges would like to have my job,
but they can only roll, not fly.

My grandmother had a pear tree right behind her house. In the 50s, her garden was nationalized and turned into an abandoned lot. The tree remembered the garden and sprouted only as many leaves as it needed to survive. The pears were small red tears we weren't allowed to eat.

Mommy's babies

Heere, mommy's babies, come heeere, mommy's babies! My grandmother calls the chicken in a high-pitched voice as she walks into the yard hunched, stooped under a heavy weight.

The chickens come running. She throws them handfuls of corn that glint in the air like gold beads. In the fall, she'll make a great charred chicken soup from the young red roosters she raises like her own kids.

I'll never go to heaven, she says, *because of all the children I killed.*

The children I tore out of my body are buried in the far corner
of the garden, my grandmother says. Each spring, the earth reminds me of
their presence, sending up their wide-eyed faces as violets.

His name is Johnny, Johnny-Jump-Up. I named him that because
he jumped right out of my earth-scented belly. Say Hi, Johnny.
Hi, he nods, and goes back to jump rope.

Yes

Yes yes yes.

The answer is yes.

Yes: in fall, the leaves get their yellow passports and emigrate from the trees.
They all look for a better life in Dirtland, but very few make it there.
Most of them are blown down the street by the fall wind. That's how I got
here, my dear.

Yes: every church on earth has a mirror church in the sky. This is true for
mosques, too. The churches hang upside down and float over mountains and
fields, while cardinals toll the bells.

Yes: an orange lily hangs from the sky. Its pistil drips the noon light on earth
until the hummingbird sticks its tongue inside and drinks.

No

No, the rose is naked under her red dress. Tonight her scent reminds
me of an old street where we walked toward the flower's center, its secret
stamens and sweet erect pistil. We didn't talk, for fear the pollen would fall into
our mouths.

No, the trees conceal their roots under a veil of dirt, the way my grandmother
wore a dark headscarf over her hair to tell the world her husband was dead.
Cloth, not words.

No, there is nothing sadder in the world than a woman waiting all her life for
her lover to return. She is my aunt Mariana.

    I'll come back for you, my uncle said forty years ago. The Iron Curtain
rose and fell, but he never came back.

If I died and didn't know it, I'd ask my grandpa's watch the time. The hands are stuck at five to five: time for tea, time for pie.

If the color yellow runs out, we'll make ash-gray bread with dust milled from centuries of ochre. We'll make bread with bluebell blue, or braided red with blood.

In Spain, where does rain get its blue feathers?

The blind man met the one with a broken leg in the apartment
at the military academy. God was on spring break, and, for two weeks,
the two guys lived in the abandoned dorm. The invalid counted the pizza
money; the blind man opened the door. Your father was the blind man, and
this is all I know.

Look at me, I'm dancing, says the smoke to the clouds.
Yes, they reply, but your feet are tied to the chimney.

Yes, the full moon forgot its sack of flour on the kitchen counter, next to the Milky Way rice. The virgin didn't notice. She was stirring the pot with the ladle and tasting the pisces.

The rice on the counter smiles all night at the rice spilled over the sky. I come downstairs to look for lost dreams by the light of its gleaming white teeth.

The rubies said to the pomegranates: We look like you, but we're alive.
If squeezed, we let out blood instead of juice.

Thursday is an old witch who comes at night and steals your speech.
Friday, an old woman saint, fishes the speech from the river and gives
it back only if you have fasted.

The oranges don't divide the sunlight in the orange tree; they sum it up.

The sea smiles at me with salt teeth, her bitter lips parted. She gives back the
trinkets she stole: bits of bones, curls of sailors' hair, shredded wings of angels.
At night, she remembers the names of the drowned and recites them to herself.

A black condor flies over your country, Pablo,
and a gray owl flies over mine.

In the dark ages, the secret police wrote all their documents in invisible ink. Thus, no victim could ever trace her torturers. Together, predators and prey retired in a resort by the sea and sang in the church choir.

I won my freedom when my seat fell off, confesses the abandoned bike. Now I can pedal everywhere I want, ringing my bell under the noses of traffic cops.

I'll never be free, sighs the post. My feet are stuck in concrete, and people always chain me to their bikes or dogs. Soon, I'll be a pile of rust and never see the field at dusk.

Dearest little one,

a hummingflower flies from bird to bird,
sipping sweet songs from their throats.

Taste me later rather than sooner, sings the bone in the stew.
Suck my marrow for a taste of spring grass. By tomorrow, I'll hum,
and fire will bring out the choir.

      Dip a wooden spoon inside me, answers the stew. I have the
fragrance of roots and of the life of the lamb. Lift me to your lips,
and take it all in.

Yes As soon as they stop being poor, the poor forget the potato soup they used to eat. It must be something in the water they drink, the gilded spring water they buy in small bottles.

Yes

Yes, I have plenty of room for thorns, the rosebush answered.
In spring, I'll grow long arms from the ground. I'll grab the trellis
and climb, and I'll bloom on top, but only for bees and birds,
not hands. I'll swing in the breeze, my body adorned with thorns
and with the sharp pain of your wounds.

In silence I shed the leaves. It takes a long time to loosen
and lose my long dress, the lacy bra, the deep-veined stockings.
Naked by the end of November, I quiver, anticipating your hands
of snow, your cold embrace, your kiss.

A baby goat jumps from dream to dream. In my dream, it just escaped from the slaughterhouse, and its hoofed feet leave traces of blood on snow. In your dream, the bell tied around its neck rings, and rings, and brings the spring.

Tomorrow I'll leave, I told Mom, and her face paled. My heart was a cherry that stained my white blouse with its bleeding. I clung to its sweet hard pit, praying it was hard enough to help me carry on.

We talked for a long time, eating cherries in the dark, about boys, life in a far away city, and recipes for preserves. In the morning, the cherries from the bowl were gone. We saved two pits and buried them in the garden, side by side.

The closer the sun, the riper the fruits.
The riper the fruits, the brighter they glow.
Sweetness is measured in lumens; ripeness, in watts.

The sweetness of an orange is pure light, juicy, glowing
in my mouth. Sunlight drips on my chin and stains my hands
and the napkin.

Glow-in-the-dark ripe plums, apples, and peaches drip
moonlight on earth at night. A walk in the orchard is a stroll
among stars hanging on low branches. The earth moves
among gleaming planets with the crunching sound of a bug
that eats the inside of an apple.

The tired eyes look back at me from the bathroom mirror,
still foggy, despite my efforts to wipe it clean.

On my way to work, the wipers beat against the windshield.
The highway is a blur. Hundreds of cars, strange metal birds
or fish, float in the same direction. The city sucks us in.

The sun breaks through sheets of rain, and, for a moment,
I'm on the brink of understanding my life. I catch a crumb of light,
a flake, a flicker I hold with my eyes afraid to blink.

Then, the tunnel opens, and I enter the big yawn.

III

The Bank Teller's Name Is Jesus

It says on the door behind me: THIS IS NOT AN EXIT, not an exit from unlove, or from a previous life. No table for writing, only walls and a door. Behind it, an old woman combs poems out of her hair. She is not a muse, but the cleaning lady, her front teeth missing: *This is not an exit, my dear, but an entrance. Come in.*

Since their white and black feathers look the same at night,
it's hard to tell the difference between the guardian angel and
the angel of death. I make my way through the crowd with both
of them perched on my shoulders, muttering *Excuse me, Pardon me,*
cursing under my breath how heavy they are, and how soon
I'll need both.

The bank teller's name is Jesus. Somehow, that makes me feel a lot better than the FDIC-Insured sign. Jesus is a bald guy who smiles at me, counting my money with quick hands.

A faceless woman crawls on the ceiling and hides in the lamp, or in the corner, behind the red flowers. Suddenly, she launches toward me a huge slab of stone, the lid of a tomb.

I roll out of its way. Shaking, I look hard in the dark. I scrutinize the ceiling lamp and the flowers. Nothing is there. No one. And I fall asleep again as she creeps back on her hands and knees.

You spill the small black hearts onto the floor, in slow motion. They explode and run to all corners—faceted crystal beads, chocolate cockroaches scattering alive with night. Laughing, you show me your tongue, and there it is: my black heart melting, ready to be crunched.

You turn on the city lights with the strike of a match. The angels march overhead in rows that flicker and flutter, past the sandwich man who holds the sign: BEST WINGS IN TOWN. FREE DELIVERY.

Dark sheep, they shiver in the wind. Slick hair, short, stocky,
they look for work as seamstresses, construction workers, nannies.
Sometimes they laugh. Sometimes they look around. Some lean against
the poster in the bus stop that advertises a new show on History Channel:
America, The Story of Us.

Always, everything George
For George Vasilievici, 1978-2010

George passes by the beggar child who cries coins on the sidewalk.
His room upstairs has four walls, four entrances and no exit. The moths
pour from the mattress into his mouth. George juliennes his onion love,
tears streaming down his face.

     In the hallway, he sees his own mother carrying him in her womb
in a red lacquered casket. On the balcony, George laughs at himself:
the tall awkward tassel dangling at the end of the scarf.

Place your left foot on the folded wings, and your right one on the tied legs. Grab the head with your left hand, and, with your right, slide the blunt knife across the stretched neck until the skin gives in and life drips into the ground.

No screech will escape your fist, no cry, the eyes half-covered by papery lids, wings fighting, legs trying to outrun death. Hold the twitching neck stump down so the blood won't spill and spatter the yard.

Look up and smile, so proud of your first kill.

The neighborhood queen

For me, my dear, some men did the unthinkable. Like the son
of the mailman who mailed himself in a package that never reached
its destination.

When I passed by, the blackbirds whistled. The dogs barked
and rattled the fences. I danced on rooftops in mercury slippers. Midnight
was just a dress I wore, and rain was my tambourine. They called me
The Charmer and feared I'd give them the deadly quicksilver. I laughed
at them, shaking my copper hair.

One day, a crow came down from the church's steeple and
placed its feet on my face. The women gasped and covered their mouths:
overnight, I was a hundred years old. And I kept dancing.

42ⁿᵈ Street Times Square

The man in a top hat blows into a noisemaker. His shadow wakes
up startled and bites his leg. *Boy, are my arms tired of flying*, mutters
the suitcase a girl pulls through the crowd. The preacher rolls his eyes
and yells *Repent! Repent! For God is a consuming fire*—and I would,
but my train has arrived.

On the 7 train, some people would obviously be played by certain actors: There is the Tom Wilkinson guy, the Delroy Lindo guy, the William H. Macy guy. Frances McDormand's daughter, played by a tired Reese Witherspoon, had just given up her baby for adoption. They look in silence through the grimy windows to the city that grows strange and new across the river.

My lover Daniel Day Lewis waits for me in Grand Central. As the train runs into the tunnel, I think of his dry hands, his windblown eyes. Later, I walk through the crowd toward the clock and someone plays a heartbreaking 70's saxophone as I see him kissing another Juliette Binoche.

On CNN tonight, the story of a woman hiker lost in the Alps. She was saved from certain death by a helicopter. The crew said to the camera: *She told us we were her angels sent from heavens to save her. We almost didn't see her, but she signaled to the helicopter with her red sports bra. Her bare breasts were so bright, like lighthouses, like blinding mirrors. That's when we saw her, and we made our descent.*

The 6 p.m. news

The largest hummus ever made broke the Guinness World record,
but the chefs who made it didn't have a bowl large enough to present it.
They contacted a satellite company to use one of their dishes as a bowl.
For next year, the chefs are planning to break a new record: the world's
largest cabbage pickled in the Hubble telescope.

The only regret I have, says the bank robber in the getaway car, is that
I didn't steal the heart of the beautiful teller named Maria Magdalene.

At rush hour, the highway is packed with buses and cars carrying potatoes,
not people. The skins crackle in the sun, and traffic cooks slowly as goulash.
To pass the time, the drivers whistle, but the potatoes can only blink.

Myths flying low over the city

The red signs on the couple's foreheads show something cosmic or magical. They sell newspapers. She wears a green sari and says with an accent: *Daily Nuuzz*. They don't know Mahabharata, Ramayana, The Vedic Hymns. They just try to stay afloat in the rushed sea of people in Penn Station.

You pick up the paper and give her the coins. You look at the poster in the bus stop, thinking Lancelot must be a football player. The Iranian man from the souvenir store couldn't care less about Gilgamesh's songs. The Greek taxi driver doesn't give a damn about the river Styx when he takes us over Queensborough Bridge.

In the cab, we don't speak. I look up and see an old Phoenix flying over 7th Avenue, flapping its wings over buses and cars. A feather drops at the traffic light. The Phoenix turns Macy's corner with a shriek, then up to its nest on top of the Empire State Building. We still don't speak. The bird sets itself on fire, and no one notices.

The violinist plays with his arms on fire. Soon the velvet curtains catch the flames from his bow, but no one moves: the audience is roped to the chairs, their mouths stuffed with cotton. On the painted ceiling, the angels clap and whistle.

I carry small animals in the pockets of my bathrobe: a monkey,
a deer, a rabbit, a pig. Sometimes they quarrel; sometimes they sing.
In one of my slippers, a mouse recites my latest poem.

Dressed in pink and bees, the weeping cherry gets married
to the neighbors' much older oak tree. I am the priest, rake in hand,
dirty knees. Daffodil bells ring. *You may kiss the bride*, I mutter,
and something gets in my eyes.

I skate on the rim of the half-empty glass. Under my feet,
thin skins of sound peel from the edge and lift into the air.
The hand raises the glass to the light. The nose sniffs the wine.
The wrist gives it a whirl. Where would I rather fall: into the
abyss of the floor, or into the dark mouth that waits?

I finally got inside the ear and told my story to the dwarf.
The dwarf listened politely, then took my story to the anvil
and beat out all the details with his hammer. He gave my story
a serial number, walked over a spiral corridor, then climbed
a ladder to a thickly-padded room and placed it on a shelf
next to another million stories. *What did you do to it?* I yelled.
It was the story of my life! It doesn't belong to you anymore,
the dwarf said. It will be very happy here in the music room
where all the stories play all day on a set of broken eardrums.

She comes in from the rain and hangs her jacket made from a flock
of birds on the coat rack. At the table, she eats her cereal studded
with lucky charms. She eats the locket and key, the swirl stars,
the golden fish who grants her three wishes. She eats the horseshoe,
the four-leaved clover, the silver cross.

    Do you have any more charms, Mom? she asks.

    This is the last one, I tell her, and take the chimneysweeper
out of the box. His small red heart still twinkles when she places him
into her mouth.

A man walks through murky knee-high water, carrying a large mirror.
The mirror has a bright yellow frame and is very heavy, so he stops,
places it on his head, then resumes walking. He walks uphill against
the current, toward the end of the devastated street, now a gray river.
On his head, he balances the dim glass sheet in which he can see
his entire life and the faces of the 160 people dead in the deluge.

Things I know about angels

They are afraid of dark and dogs, afraid of being afraid. Sometimes,
they lose the golden trumpets and can't announce to the world the birth
of another savior.

      Sometimes, they get stuck in traffic. When they see the ambulance
lights and neighbors talk quietly, shaking their heads, the angels know they
have arrived too late.

      And, if they don't meet the quota of saved suicides and near-miss
accidents, they get clouded: no TV, no dinner, no singing in the choir.
They turn in the wings and halos, and get assigned to desk duty at the asylum.

      That's what Peter told me one cold night, Peter, the angel
in a wheelchair, almost petrified by frost, panhandling at the corner
of 31st and 1st.

I rang the doorbell at the top floor apartment

Come in, she gestures from the mirror as she combs her long gray hair. She closes the door behind me, and I walk carefully through smoke, through raining bombs across the living room devoured by flames.

      Shhhh, the old woman says, placing a bony finger over her lips. *Take a seat. Peel an apple. Write a poem if you wish, but don't say a word, no matter what you see. Shhhh, mankind is sleeping.*

Longbeak

Longbeak could pluck a cherry of fire from the tree that grows
at the center of the earth. He could find a pearl in the ocean
and my earring lost in the pitch-black sewer. Longbeak had tall
robot legs and a metal crane body. He could build a skyscraper
overnight, even an entire city in which no one lived. When his
work was done, he let out a shriek, hoping someone would hear it.
      Longbeak got lonely when the construction workers left.
No one loved him. No one talked to him, except the clouds that
mumbled in his ear. Longbeak stretched his neck and tapped
his long beak on the moon, a closed door in the sky. Knock-knock.
No one answered. He went back and built another empty city.

Off a tin roof

Just before nightfall,
the last angel I knew

flew off
a tin roof

without a parachute
or wings

and never reached
the street

A girl's hand is a dandelion. It stretches from the ground, soft fingers spread out, slightly blurry in the spring light. The breeze blows the dandelion seeds away. Little fingers float, parachute in new yards, in new grass, growing other dandelions, girl hands waving from the ground.

Notes & Bibliography

*There's something I must tell you,/ but you don't have to listen./ Of turtle's wings
and sticky things/ and a tooth of mine that's missing./ Come close so I can
whisper/ things I don't understand./ And, as I tell my tales/for naughty boys and
girls,/ please, may I hold your hand?*
Epigraph from Duane Michals' *Upside Down Inside Out and Backwards*
© Duane Michals 1993, A Sonny Boy Book.

The snake
The poem was inspired by the Romanian myth of the twin brother gods
Brother (Fartatul) and Unbrother (Nefartatul) as described by Romulus
Vulcanescu in *Romanian Mythology/Mitologie Romana*, Editura Academiei,
Bucharest, 1987, pgs. 245-246.

The half-man-half-a-limp-rabbit is a malefic character in many Romanian
folk tales.

The stag
This poem is inspired by the Christmas carol about a mythical stag that
carries baby Jesus in a silk swing in its antlers (Romulus Vulcanescu,
Romanian Mythology, Editura Academiei, Bucharest, 1987, pg. 510.)

Gaia
Gaia is a predator bird from the order *Falconiformes*. According to
Romanian folklore, the bird personifies the death goddess and follows
humans everywhere, flying in circles overhead.
(*Ion Ghinoiu, Small Encyclopedia of Romanian Traditions/Mica enciclopedie de
traditii romanesti*, Editura Agora, Bucharest, 2008, pg. 127.)

*Will our life not be a tunnel/ between two vague clarities?/ Or will it not be a
clarity/ between two dark triangles?/ Or will life not be a fish/ prepared to be a
bird?*
Epigraph from Pablo Neruda's *The Book of Questions,* Copper Canyon Press,
1991, 2001, translated by William O'Daly.

Always, everything George borrows and collages fragments from the long
poem *Always, everything (De toate, mereu)* by George Vasilievici.
My translation of *Always, everything* was published by *The Exquisite Corpse.*
Rest in peace, George, and may the Muse be with you.

About the Author

Claudia Serea is a Romanian-born poet who immigrated to the U.S. in 1995. Her poems and translations have appeared in *5 a.m., Meridian, Harpur Palate, Word Riot, Blood Orange Review, Cutthroat, Green Mountains Review, Connotation Press: An Online Artifact,* and many others.

A two-time nominee for the Pushcart Prize and Best of the Net, she is the author of two other full-length collections: *To Part Is to Die a Little* (Červená Barva Press), and *A Dirt Road Hangs from the Sky* (8th House Publishing, Montréal, Canada). She also published the chapbooks *Eternity's Orthography* (Finishing Line Press, 2007) and *With the Strike of a Match* (White Knuckles Press, 2011).

Together with Paul Doru Mugur and Adam J. Sorkin, Serea recently co-edited and co-translated *The Vanishing Point That Whistles, an Anthology of Contemporary Romanian Poetry* (Talisman House, 2011). Another book of translations is Adina Dabija's *Beautybeast,* forthcoming from NorthShore Press.

Claudia Serea is one of the founders of the poetry group The Red Wheelbarrow Poets in Rutherford, New Jersey, and art directs their journal *The Red Wheelbarrow.* She lives in New Jersey and works in New York for a major publishing company.

About Phoenicia Publishing

Phoenicia Publishing is a small independent press based in Montreal but involved, through a network of online connections, with writers and artists all over the world. We are interested in words and images that illuminate culture, spirit, and the human experience. A particular focus is on writing and art about travel between cultures—whether literally, through lives of refugees, immigrants, and travelers, or more metaphorically and philosophically—with the goal of enlarging our understanding of one another through universal and particular experiences of change, displacement, disconnection, assimilation, sorrow, gratitude, longing and hope.

We are committed to the innovative use of the web and digital technology in all aspects of publishing and distribution, and to making high-quality works available that might not be viable for larger publishers. We work closely with our authors, and are pleased to be able to offer them a greater share of royalties than is normally possible.

Your support of this endeavor is greatly appreciated.

Our complete catalogue is online at www.phoeniciapublishing.com

www.ingramcontent.com/pod-product-compliance
Lightning Source LLC
LaVergne TN
LVHW051701080426
835511LV00017B/2675